BodyOpolis and the Vitamin Hero

ADMIRAL

Written by
Karen Ullery

Illustrated by
Dana J. Sullivan

Life's Energy
with Karen

Kirkland, Washington

This book series is dedicated to God
(Source, Creator, Divine Love, Universal Flow, the Force …
whatever one chooses to call it).
Thank you for being a constant wellspring of love and
inspiration and for this miraculous download! May we uplift,
unify and bring wellness to all with this little sprinkle of love!
— K.U.

To Mother Nature.
Thanks for all the food!
— D.J.S

Published by
Life's Energy With Karen LLC
11733 Holmes Point Drive NE
Kirkland, WA 98034
BodyOpolis.com

First Edition, 2017

ISBN: 978-0-9990949-0-7

No, it's not up in space.

It's closer to you than you might even know,

in fact, it's within you, from your head to your toe.

Using your imagination...
you will see this
inside nation!

Welcome to BodyOpolis

Pop: 137 Trillion Cells, Bacteria & Fungi

Turn the page
and you will see
this city
working perfectly!

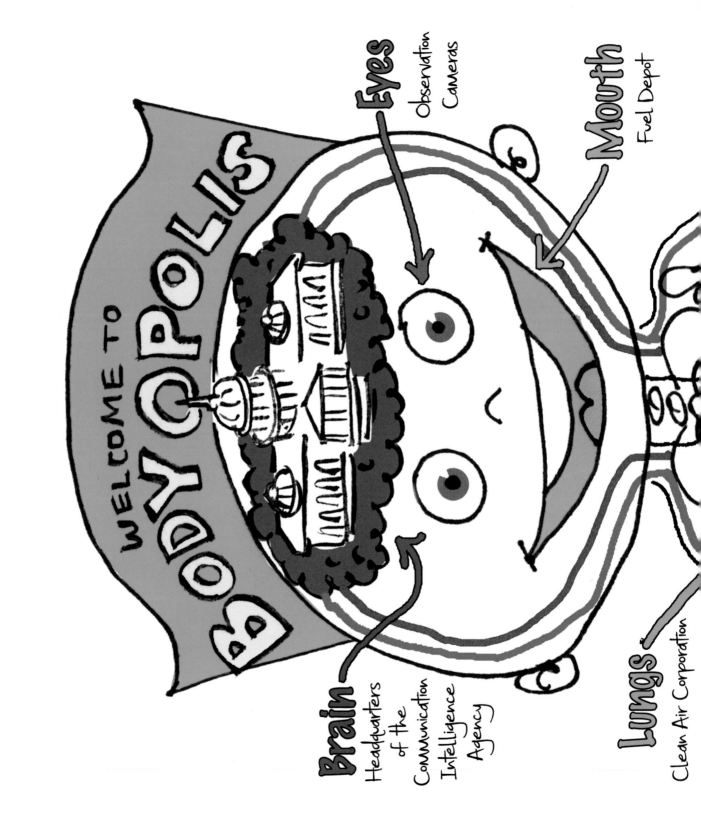

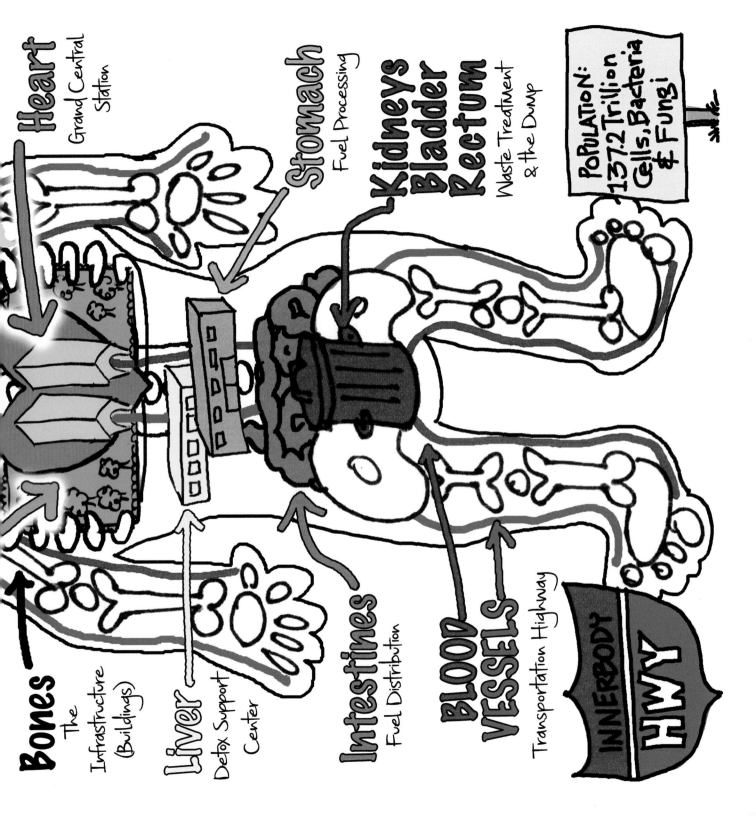

Heart Grand Central Station

Stomach Fuel Processing

Kidneys Bladder Rectum Waste Treatment & the Dump

POPULATION: 137.2 Trillion Cells, Bacteria & Fungi!

Bones The Infrastructure (Buildings)

Liver Detox Support Center

Intestines Fuel Distribution

BLOOD VESSELS Transportation Highway

INNERBODY HWY

To keep BodyOpolis working just right,
   proper fuel is delivered with every bite.

See,
YOU are the source that
   feeds this fine city,
   so let's get right down to
      the nitty gritty.

Deep
in the city,
when you search
you will find,
many helpers
and heroes
of every kind!
Today you will meet,
let there be no delay,
a hero who's known as
Admiral A!

Admiral A knows his job is very serious,

and part of his role is
ultra mysterious.

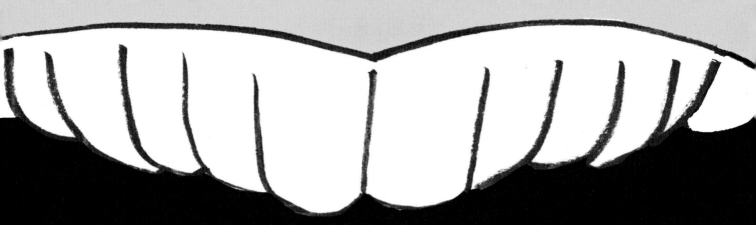

He strengthens your fuel crushers (every sort)
that break down your food to prepare for transport.

He works to keep all of your buildings quite strong,
so they can protect your city lifelong.

He maintains your cameras that see and detect,
all the outside events; to keep them in check.

He also makes sure that
your external walls,
are healthy and strong
and shield you from falls.

These outside walls provide great protection,
so the city stays safe and free from infection.

He supports the security
team that is quick,
to fight off invaders
that can make you sick.

SHH...

Now let's take a look
at his secretive role,
the one where his duty
is damage control.

Admiral A is part of an elite special group,
that fights off free radicals in one mighty swoop.

Free radicals are confused
and unbalanced creatures,
who can damage the city
and some of its features.

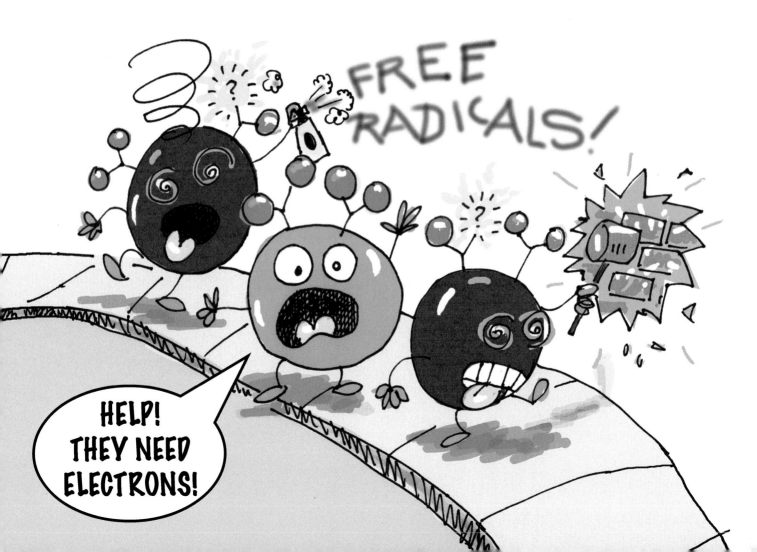

Antioxidant Super Heroes,
or A.S.H. as they're known,
fix these free radicals and set
a good tone.

Now you might be impressed with Admiral A,
but he's nothing unless his supply's on the way.

So let's make it clear right here in this hour,
that YOU are the one who holds all the power!

The fuel you feed to your city each day,
delivers the power of Admiral A.

So let's break it down and develop a plan,
so Admiral A will do all that he can.

Admiral A

The Liver, Suite 100, BodyOpolis, YOU

A, Admiral

EXPERIENCES AND SKILLS

- **Maintenance:** Helps maintain healthy bones, teeth, skin and eyes.

- **Builder:** Assists cell division and renewal to keep the body growing and as good as new.

- **Supporter:** Boosts the immune system to keep the body healthy and strong.

MEMBERSHIP

- **Antioxidant Super Heroes:** Neutralize and balance free radicals that can damage the body as they search for their missing electron.

FAVORITE FOOD

- Admiral A needs **FAT**. Without it, he loses power and can't be absorbed, transported, converted or stored.

- Admiral A is stored in the **liver** and **fat cells** until he is needed.

- Admiral A performs best with **Vitamins B, D and E,** and **Minerals, Calcium, Zinc** and **Phosphorus.**

ADMIRAL A SUPER FO

 Cantaloupe

 Mango

 Carrot

 Peach

 Apricot

 Sweet Potato

 Papaya

 Nectarine

 Kale

 Broccoli

 Avocado

Pineapple

can you find these Super Foods throughout the book?

 Watermelon

 Pumpkin

 Fish

 Goji Berries

 Prune

 Milk

These foods are rich in Vitamin A!

ODS FOR SUPER KIDS

 Beet & Leaves

 Spinach

Tomato

 Swiss Chard

Bell Pepper

 Egg

Yellow Squash

 Cod Liver Oil

Food is best when it's fresh and whole. It's good for your body and great for your soul!

FUEL UP WITH

Admiral A Super Salad

Chop and Mix 1/2 Cup of any of the following:

- Papaya
- Cantaloupe
- Nectarine
- Mango
- Avocado
- Peaches
- Apricots

Admiral A Super Smoothie

Mix in Blender (fresh or frozen)

1 cup Strawberries

1 cup Mango

1 cup Packed Spinach

1/2 Ripe Banana

1/4 cup Yogurt

3/4 cup Coconut Milk or Pineapple Juice

2 T. Chia Seeds

ADMIRAL A!

Admiral A Flower Power!

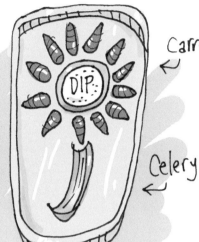

Carrots

Celery

Favorite Dip
Baby Carrots
Celery

I'm quite the food artist!

Admiral A's Honey Bear

4 slices Kiwi Fruit
8 raw Almonds
4 Blueberries
Top & bottom of a Banana
   (for eyes)
Cantaloupe in these shapes
Honey drizzle (for smile)

GROWING STRONG

Grow your own Admiral A Window Garden

Needed:

- Sunny Window Sill
- Deep Pot(s)
- Potting Soil
- Baby Carrot Seeds
- Regular Water
- Loving Care

GET CREATIVE!

Share YOUR Ideas
on
BodyOpolis.com
and meet ALL the Vitamin Heroes!

Made in the USA
Lexington, KY
05 September 2017